D0120304

C153227225

Animal Lives

ORANG-UTANS

Sally Morgan

QED Publishing

Copyright © QED Publishing 2006

First published in the UK in 2006 by
QED Publishing
A Quarto Group company
226 City Road
London EC1V 2TT

www.qed-publishing.co.uk

All rights reserved. No part of this publication
may be reproduced, stored in a retrieval
system, or transmitted in any form or by any
means, electronic, mechanical, photocopying,
recording, or otherwise, without the prior
permission of the publisher, nor be otherwise
circulated in any form of binding or cover
other than that in which it is published and
without a similar condition being imposed
on the subsequent purchaser.

A Catalogue record for this book is
available from the British Library.

ISBN 1 84538 379 6

Written by Sally Morgan
Editor Hannah Ray
Designed by Jonathan Vipond
Picture Researcher Joanne Forrest Smith

Publisher Steve Evans
Art Director Zeta Davies
Editorial Director Jean Coppendale

Printed and bound in China

KENT
LIBRARIES & ARCHIVES
C153227225

Picture Credits

Key: t=top, b=bottom, l=left, r=right,
c=centre, FC=front cover

Corbis/Tom Brakefield 4–5, 12–13, 23, /Chris
Hellier 24, /Renee Lynn 14, /D Robert & Lorri
Franz 9, 16; **FLPA**/Konrad Wothe/Minden
Pictures 18, /Gerry Ellis/Minden Pictures 22,
26, /David Hosking 25, /Frans Lanting
/Minden Pictures 28–29, 30cr, /Colin
Marshall 19; **Getty Images**/Tim Davis 20–21,
/Gallo Images/Heinrich van den Berg 11,
/Mark Newman 30bc, /Anup Shah FC & 1,
/Manoj Shah 27; **NHPA**/Ernie Janes 10,
/Andy Rouse 6–7, 30tc; **OSF**/Bob Bennett 15;
Still Pictures/John Cancalosi 8, /COMPOST
17, /Evelyn Gallardo 21br.

Words in **bold** are
explained in the
Glossary on page 31.

Contents

The orang-utan

The orang-utan is one of our closest relatives and is also one of the largest animals that can climb trees. It is a type of **primate**. Other primates include gorillas, monkeys, chimpanzees and humans.

The orang-utan also belongs to a group of animals called **mammals**. Other mammals include tigers, sheep, horses and giraffes. Mammals are animals that usually have hair and give birth to live young. Mammal mothers produce milk to feed their young.

The large body of the orang-utan is covered in long, orange-red hair.

Orang-utan

In Malay, the word 'orang' means man and 'utan' means forest or woods, so orang-utan means 'man of the woods'.

fact

Long arms

Orang-utans have very long arms. In fact, the length of each arm is about the same as the height of a five-year-old child. The distance from a fingertip on one hand to a fingertip on the other hand can be as much as 2.3m.

Orang-utans are intelligent animals that live in **rainforests**. Sadly, their homes are being destroyed so there is only a small number left in the world.

Where do you find orang-utans?

Orang-utans were once found across South-east Asia. Today, they are found scattered throughout the islands of Sumatra and Borneo. Borneo is a large island made up of several countries. Orang-utans can be found on Borneo in west, east and central Kalimantan, Sarawak and Sabah.

Orang-utan

Fossils of orang-utans dating back 40 000 years show that they used to be about one-third larger than they are today.

fact

Orang-utans move around the rainforest by climbing along branches.

Sumatran orang-utans
Bornean orang-utans

BRUNEI
SABAH
SARAWAK
B O R N E O
KALIMANTAN

S U M A T R A

ASIA
PACIFIC
OCEAN
AFRICA
INDIAN OCEAN
AUSTRALIA
SOUTHERN
OCEAN

I N D I A N
O C E A N

Rainforest homes

Orang-utans live in rainforests. These are dense forests found in parts of the world where the climate is hot and wet for much of the year. The trees in a rainforest grow close together and their upper leaves and branches form a leafy 'roof' called a **canopy**. The canopy blocks out the light, so the forest floor is dark and there are few plants.

The greatest numbers of orang-utans are found in the trees of the lowland swamp areas of rainforests, where there are many streams and muddy areas.

7

Orang-utan types

There is only one **species**, or type, of orang-utan. A male orang-utan is about 1.4m tall and weighs up to 80kg. That is twice as heavy as a female orang-utan. Once a male reaches the age of 14, he starts to grow an enormous pouch under his throat which he uses to make calls. He also grows cheek pads, made up mostly of fat.

Adult males have facial hair that looks like a man's moustache and beard.

Orang-utan

Some people think that the face of an orang-utan looks very like a human face.

fact

8

Two subspecies

There are some differences between orang-utans that live in Borneo and those that live on the nearby island of Sumatra, so the species is divided into two **subspecies**.

Sumatran orang-utans have a long, narrow face and thicker, longer hair than orang-utans from Borneo. Bornean orang-utans have a rounder face. Their cheek pads grow forwards, giving the face a **concave** shape.

Sumatran orang-utans, like these, are lighter in colour than orang-utans from Borneo.

Beginning life

A female orang-utan is ready to have a baby when she is about ten years old. She is **pregnant** for about nine months, the same time as a human. She gives birth to one baby that weighs about a kilogram – that's the same as a bag of sugar.

A baby orang-utan drinks its mother's milk until it is three or four years old.

Carried around

A female orang-utan carries her baby everywhere for the first year of its life. When it reaches about two years of age, the young orang-utan is allowed to explore a little on its own, but it never strays too far from its mother. The mother continues to carry her youngster on longer journeys until it is four years old.

This baby clings to its mother's fur as she climbs a tree.

Orang-utan

A female orang-utan has a baby every seven to eight years. She only has two or three babies in her lifetime.

fact

Growing up

Once a young orang-utan reaches three years of age, it starts to eat fruits and other foods. It learns which foods are safe to eat and where to find them by watching its mother. Now, the youngster is ready to start exploring. It has to learn to find its way around the forest in search of different foods.

Making friends

Over the next few years, the youngster spends longer periods of time alone. Sometimes, young orang-utans between the ages of four and seven are seen together. They play and travel with each other for a while. This is part of their preparation for leaving their mother and living on their own. By the age of seven or eight, an orang-utan is ready to look after itself.

Orang-utan fact

Orang-utans help to scatter the seeds of rainforest plants. As they eat, they spit out the larger seeds. These seeds drop to the forest floor where they grow into new plants.

These two youngsters
are playing together
in the forest.

13

Living alone

Orang-utans live alone in the rainforest. The only time they live with other orang-utans is when they are growing up, when a young female returns to visit her mother or when a male visits a female to mate with her. This is different from other primates, such as chimpanzees and gorillas, who live together in small groups.

Orang-utans spend most of their lives alone in the trees.

Home range

Orang-utans move around a particular area of the forest, called their **home range**. Sometimes, female orang-utans that live in the same area meet each other. However, they generally make little contact and go their separate ways.

When male orang-utans meet, they make a lot of noise and charge at one another to try and scare each other away. If this doesn't work, they bite each other.

Orang-utan fact

Female orang-utans are attracted to males with large cheek pads.

Male orang-utans show their teeth as a threat to other males.

Daily routines

Orang-utans do the same things each day. They wake up at dawn and are active for two or three hours, moving around the forest looking for food. The middle of the day is usually hot, so the orang-utans rest in the high branches of trees or in a simple nest. They are active again during the afternoon, when they move though the forest, feeding all the time.

Orang-utans move slowly and rarely travel than one kilometre in a day.

Making nests

During the early evening, an orang-utan looks for a place to make its nest for the night. The nest is made from leaves and twigs and takes about five minutes to make. The females and young orang-utans build their nests about 12 to 18m high in the trees. The adult males are much heavier, so they usually build their nests on the forest floor.

Orang-utan nests look like large birds' nests.

Orang-utan fact

If it is raining, orang-utans build a roof of leaves and branches over their nests to keep themselves dry.

17

Feeding

This young orang-utan is watching and learning from its mother.

Orang-utans have to eat vast quantities to survive, so they spend as much as half the day searching for food. Sometimes, they spend a whole day sitting in a tree, gorging themselves on its fruit.

Plant eaters

Orang-utans eat mostly plant food. Their favourite food is fruit, and this makes up more than half of their diet. They know the location of many different fruit trees in the forest and when the trees are due to produce fruits. As well as fruit, orang-utans also eat young leaves, shoots, tree bark, insects, birds' eggs and honey.

Mother orang-utans show their young where to find fruit.

Orang-utan

By the time an orang-utan is ten years old, it can identify about 200 different food plants.

fact

Moving through the trees

Orang-utans move slowly from tree to tree, using their long arms. Sometimes, they come down to the ground to walk to the next tree. However, it is safer in the trees, where they are out of reach of **predators** such as tigers and leopards.

The hands and feet of orang-utans are hook-shaped to make it easier to grab branches. Their thumbs and big toes stick out at an angle to make it easier for them to grip and pick up objects.

Young orang-utans
can swing from
branch to branch
and travel quickly
through the forest.

Orang-utans
tend to walk on
all fours, with a
side-to-side shuffle.
They use their fists
for support.

21

Orang-utan senses

Orang-utans have very similar senses to humans: hearing, sight, smell, taste and touch. They need to use all of their senses to survive in the forest. They have good hearing and listen for other animals moving around the forest, especially predators. They also listen for the calls of other orang-utans. They use their sense of smell to find food.

Young orang-utans use their sense of touch when they play with each other.

Like humans and other primates, orang-utans can see in colour.

Orang-utan

Orang-utans love to eat a fruit called a durian. It is very smelly. The smell helps the orang-utans to find the fruit in the forest.

fact

Seeing in the forest

Orang-utans have eyes that are positioned close together so that they can see in 3D. This enables orang-utans to judge how far away things are, which is important when they are moving through the trees and reaching out to pick fruits. However, the forest is dark and it is not possible to see long distances. This means the orang-utan has to rely on its other senses to detect other animals in the forest.

Intelligent animals

Orang-utans are intelligent animals. They have learned to use 'tools' made from bits of twig to scratch themselves, to dig and to collect food. For example, the seeds of a fruit called a puwin are very tasty but the fruit itself is prickly and painful to hold. Orang-utans have learned to use a stick to pull out the seeds without hurting their hands.

This adult male is using a twig to clean his teeth.

Orang-utans build a shelter from leaves to hide under during wet weather.

Other tools

Leaves are also used as tools. Orang-utans may use leaves to collect drinking water. Some orang-utans have even been seen using leaves as napkins, to wipe juice from their chins!

Copying people

Orang-utans are very good at copying people. Orang-utans living in rescue centres in Malaysia have learned to untie boats from their moorings and ride them across a river!

Orang-utan fact

One female orang-utan used 54 tools for hunting insects and 20 tools for getting fruit.

Communication

Orang-utans use sounds to communicate. Although they live alone, they recognize the calls of other orang-utans that live in the same area.

Adult males make a very loud roar, or bellow. They make this call to keep other males away and to let females know that they are in the area.

Male orang-utans use their throat pouches to make their roars louder.

Orang-utan fact

An orang-utan called Chantek was taught sign language. He learned about 140 signs and signed mainly about food!

Other calls

Other calls include a 'squeak' and 'grumph' sound that orang-utans make when they are disturbed. When they are annoyed, orang-utans break off branches and throw them down to the ground in anger!

Youngsters whine when they need help from their mother.

Orang-utans under threat

One hundred years ago, there were 300 000 orang-utans in the world. Now there are just 30 000. There is a chance that, in just 30 years' time, orang-utans may become **extinct** and disappear forever.

One reason for the steep fall in numbers is the loss of their rainforest **habitat**. The forests are being cleared for timber, new farmland and for settlements.

Orang-utans are also popular pets in some parts of Asia. Female orang-utans are killed and their babies are sold as pets.

Conservation

The only way to save the orang-utan is to protect the rainforests. Some rainforests in Borneo and Sumatra have been made into national parks and all the wildlife living in the forests is protected. There are also charities that rescue pet orang-utans.

Special centres in
Borneo teach rescued
orang-utans how to live
in the forest again.

Life cycle

A female orang-utan is ready to have a baby by about 10 years of age. She gives birth to a baby every 7 to 8 years. A male orang-utan is ready to breed by about 12 years of age, but continues to develop its cheek pads and throat pouch until it is about 20 years old. An orang-utan may live for between 40 and 45 years in the wild, and as many as 60 years in captivity.

Baby

Juvenile

Adult male

Glossary

canopy a cover of leaves and branches that shades the rainforest floor

concave rounded inwards, like the inside of a bowl

extinct no longer in existence, disappeared completely

habitat the place in which an animal or plant lives

home range an area where an orang-utan spends its life

mammal an animal that is covered in hair and gives birth to live young, rather than laying eggs. Female mammals produce milk to feed their young

predator an animal that hunts other animals

pregnant a female animal that has a baby, or babies, developing inside her

primate a type of mammal such as monkey, ape, lemur or human that has hands and feet and a large brain

rainforest dense forest found in hot and wet parts of the world

species a group of animals that look alike and can breed together to produce young

subspecies groups within a species that look slightly different from each other

Index